FRIDA KAHLO

FRIDA KAHLO

Frank Milner

PRC

This edition first published in 2001 by
PRC Publishing Ltd,
64 Brewery Road, London N7 9NT

A member of **Chrysalis** Books plc

© 1995 PRC Publishing Ltd.
Reprinted 2002

ISBN 1 85648 614 1

Printed and bound in China

Page 1
Still Life with Parrot, 1951
Harry Ransom Humanities
Research Center Art Collection
University of Texas, Austin, TX
(66.7)

Page 2
Self-Portrait with Monkey, 1938
Bequest of A. Conger Goodyear,
1966
Albright-Knox Art Gallery,
Buffalo, NY

Page 4
Naturaleza Viva, 1952
Private Collection

Page 5
Self-Portrait: The Frame, 1938
Musée National d'Art Moderne,
Paris

CONTENTS

INTRODUCTION

Paradoxically, the thread that runs through Frida Kahlo's immensely personal art is a polemical one. From her halting pictures of the mid-1920s, to the unfinished portrait of Stalin which she painted through a haze of pain-killing drugs just prior to her death in 1954, Kahlo's oeuvre of just over 140 pictures is predominantly an outward and visible manifestation of some strongly held belief. The subject matter is occasionally public in subject, although more usually private, but a propagandist edge is rarely completely absent. Ultimately it is this political dimension that underpins the popularity of Kahlo's art today. Her pictures were collected during her own lifetime, especially by the select group of admirers and friends in the United States and Mexico, but since the late 1970s her art, available in reproduction and shown in exhibitions throughout the world, has taken on an enormously enhanced stature.

Frida Kahlo is widely regarded as the most important twentieth-century woman artist in the Americas. Her reputation among feminist cultural historians is almost iconic; her confessional paintings, full of symbols of physical pain, humiliation and fortitude, have struck a particular chord among the heterodox advocates of the late-twentieth-century politics of the personal. Kahlo's provocative self-display of her mutilations has led many commentators to view her pictures as more generally symbolic of female struggle in a world of patriarchal domination. Her bisexual freedom, and the series of lovers that included Leon Trotsky and the film-star Dolores del Rio, has endowed Kahlo with added glamour. There are times when the fusion of wit, sex, seriousness, suffering and narcissism in her work makes her seem more like certain contemporary pop stars. It perhaps comes as no surprise that Madonna is one of her greatest fans.

Kahlo's earliest political enthusiasms centered upon the Mexican Revolution, the first great revolutionary upheaval of the twentieth century. She even lied about her birth in order to have people believe that she had been born in 1910, the altogether more romantic year of the Revolution's beginning, rather than 1907, the year of her actual birth. Kahlo grew up as the Revolution unfolded. Consolidation of revolutionary changes – and stability in Mexican political life – was not achieved until the mid-1920s. As a student in Mexico City, she attended the prestigious National Preparatory School where, from 1922, she was at the very heart of an educational reforming climate that had been fostered by the radical Minister of Education, José Vasconcelos. Vasconcelos was responsible for largescale programs of school and library building, and a massive literacy drive among the rural poor. Kahlo's privileged

Left Kahlo's studio with the unfinished portrait of Stalin that she was working on at the time of her death in July 1954.

Right Kahlo's elaborately coiffed hair was used symbolically in certain portraits to express the state of her relationship with Rivera.

education (she was one of 35 girls among 2000 students), intended to lead to her becoming one of the few female doctors in Mexico, was at the apex of this pyramid of national educational improvement. One of the more idiosyncratic features of Vasconcelos's educational reforms in the arts was his commissioning of murals to decorate public buildings, including the walls of Kahlo's own school. Among the artists who worked on the paintings at her school from 1921 was the 36-year-old Diego Rivera, who subsequently became Frida's husband (twice) and her lifelong companion. Although the couple were not apparently introduced to each other until several years later, both Kahlo and Rivera developed different accounts of the mutual attraction that each felt for the other, dating from a meeting they had when Kahlo was at school. This was characteristic of the retrospective myth creation that was indulged in by them both.

Murals created on public buildings by Rivera and others during the 1920s celebrated the achievements of the Mexican Revolution, as well as rather naively portraying some of the more grandiloquent hopes for the future. They also reflected much of the contradictory and conflicting nature of that extraordinary upheaval. Mexico's revolution had resulted in a government whose reforms included the breaking up of efficient agrarian capitalist estates, in order to return land to communal and village-run subsistence economics, as well as a program for modernizing industry. Trade unions were directly linked to the government by open and secret deals, and given a special protected status in exchange for co-operation. Mexico's revolution was not so much a socialist revolution (although many of its strongest supporters, including Rivera and eventually Kahlo, saw themselves as socialists), but rather a corporatist creation in which poor peasants, proletariat, the army, the middle classes and the intelligentsia were brought together into a government of national unity. With a distinctly nationalistic tone, which was anti-colonial and often anti-Western, the government's various attempts to fuse the historic and the modern were at best anti-rational, and at times downright mystical. To outsiders, like those European and North American socialist revolutionaries whose universalistic beliefs were rooted in proletarian internationalism, the Mexican Revolution seemed a perplexing compromise. It is important to understand that Kahlo's own political awareness, nurtured in such a climate, was deeply influenced by this blend of contradictory influences. The polarity of the ancient and the modern is a consistent feature of many of her self-portraits, in which she projects herself as a vibrant amalgam of the two. There is a sense in which Kahlo's oeuvre is at times paradigmatic of Mexico itself.

Frida's own family had a mixture of Mexican and European antecedents. Her father, Guillermo Kahlo, was an emigré Hungarian Jew, whose parents had fled persecution under the Austro-Hungarian Empire and settled in Europe. He arrived in Mexico aged 18, married, was widowed, put his children into an orphanage and remarried. His second wife Matilde, Frida's mother, was of mixed Mexican background – an Indian father, and a Creole mother who was the daughter of a Spanish general. Guillermo Kahlo was a photographer. His business in Mexico City combined bread-and-butter portraiture with more adventurous landscape work, including the recording for the government of ancient architectural remains. As a child, Frida was very close to her father and helped him in his studio. While

no direct connections can be established with certainty between her art and her father's photography, a childhood spent steeped in the everyday business of picture-making cannot but have helped to encourage her own confidence in that direction.

Above Kahlo and Rivera at the 1933 exhibition of Jewish portraits held to protest against Nazi antisemitism.

Left Following his dismissal by Rockefeller, Rivera worked on murals attacking political repression in the United States.

Above right Polychromed clay devotional figure of the Massacre of the Innocents, the type of popular, visceral imagery that fed into Kahlo's own art.

Right One of Kahlo's elaborately painted plastercasts, which she wore for months after one of her many operations.

THE ACCIDENT

The dreadful, near-fatal accident that happened to Kahlo when she was 18 transformed her life. In September, 1925, she was going home from central Mexico City, when the bus in which she was traveling was crushed by a tramcar. She was thrown from the wreckage and her spine, pelvis, foot and collar bone were all broken in numerous places and a metal handrail pierced through her pelvis. Several others were killed in the crash and Kahlo was not expected to live. Although she had been a diminutive child, never very strong, and already had one atrophied leg as a result of polio, there had been no reason to expect that she would not fulfil her ambition to train in medicine. Now, however, she became a semi-invalid and during the remainder of her life underwent over 30 operations, often requiring protracted periods of convalescence, when she was fitted into constricting plaster corsets. Her injuries may also have contributed to her inability to carry a child full-term, and she subsequently had three abortions. Hospitals, operations, the intimate diagrammatic depiction of human organs as though laid out for dissection, all later feed into the art of Frida Kahlo and become one of the most distinctive parts of her personal iconography.

Kahlo became an artist through her accident. During her initial convalescence she painted with pigments which her father used for coloring in and retouching photographs. 'Nothing,' she said, 'seemed more normal than to paint what had not been fulfilled.' Her first pictures, however, were not focused on her own losses but were portraits of her sisters and schoolfriends. They tend to be painted to type, three-quarter

length, with the sitter staring to the right, and the edges of face, figure and fabric hard and linear. Backgrounds are treated more as flat backdrops and left plain, with a selection of symbols indicating the interests of the portrayed figure. Shadows are rarely shown as cast, but rather as soft burred edges on the inside of a circumscribing line. This, together with her use of almond-shaped eyes and faces, suggests the classicizing conventions for drawing, painting, advertising and, importantly, photography, which were inspired by the nineteenth-century French painter Ingres and were fashionable and popular in the mid-1920s. The awkward and calculatedly 'primitive' quality of these works derives from Kahlo's sensitivity to another source, the colonial and post-colonial provincial portraiture of nineteenth-century Mexico. The naive pursuit of the sophisticated conventions of European portraiture often gave an intensity and a distinctive charm to these labored works, which might otherwise have been simply considered bad painting. Their flat and hieratic stiffness were much admired by Kahlo and she later built up a collection of these early pictures.

Kahlo is also credited with having spent a great deal of time looking through reproductions of Old Master paintings. Parallels have been drawn with Mannerist portraits, and particularly with the works of the Florentine painter Agnolo Bronzino (1503-72), whom she mentioned in one of her early letters. Again, however, the role of 1920s photographic portrait conventions should perhaps not be underestimated in the

We repudiate the so-called easel-painting and all the art of ultra-intellectual circles, because it is aristocratic, and we glorify the expression of Monumental Art because it is a public possession.

In *La Adelita, Pancho Villa and Frida*, Kahlo seems to be affirming the superiority of illustration and popular imagery over European modernisms. In the center of the picture she puts herself. Close by is a man in a lounge suit without a face. His significance is again unclear, although in this context the suit itself suggests European or, more especially, North American dress. This tension between broadly European/North American cultural mores and Mexican values is evident in other important early pictures and is quite clearly stated in Kahlo's letters. It is one of the strongest of all characteristics in her art.

Following her marriage to Diego Rivera in 1929, Kahlo spent long periods in the United States, in San Francisco, Detroit and New York. Rivera had substantial mural commissions there, and the temporary banning of the Communist party in Mexico made voluntary exile attractive for both of them. It is one of the anomalies of Rivera's life that, although he was an outspoken Communist whose subject-matter was proletarian and peasant heroics, he was employed by some of the most prominent American businessmen to decorate factories, offices, stock exchange rooms and the cultural institutions to which they subscribed. Although Kahlo made friends in the United States, she did not find the 'gringoes' to her liking, with their faces like 'uncooked cakes.' Detroit she found 'ugly and stupid;' in New York she was bored; in San Francisco she was most enamored of Chinatown.

development of her art. The photo journals of the time very often illustrated figure poses derived from sixteenth-century portraits and nineteenth-century costume pictures.

By 1927 Kahlo had gained sufficient confidence to paint a pair of pictures which represent an important broadening of her scope, and indicate her capacity to assess and tackle more avant-garde pictorial conventions. One of these includes 'Andelita' in the title, and evokes a popular Mexican song about the camp-following young woman who bewails the departure of her soldier lover. *La Adelita, Pancho Villa and Frida* shows Andelita together with one of the most swashbuckling and popular agrarian folk-heroes and leaders of the Revolution. Pancho Villa's portrait is shown hanging on a wall in the background between two larger pictures. That on the left shows revolutionary soldiers and their *soldieras* women atop a railroad waggon, awaiting transportation to battle, with Mexico's famous volcano, Popocatepetl, behind them. The picture on the right is a difficult-to-decipher view through heavily-shadowed archways across a tiled floor. It seems to be composed of Cubist and Futurist elements, and appears not to have any illustrative purpose. This in itself is probably its *raison d'être*; Kahlo appears to be contrasting one style of painting with another, narrative folk-record versus more formal modernity.

In 1927 Kahlo became a member of the Young Communist League, and she would already have been very familiar with the anti-modernist injunctions that were becoming Communist orthodoxy. She also almost certainly knew of the vow that her future husband Rivera, along with other artists, had taken in 1922 when they had set up the Mexican Union of Technical Workers, Painters and Sculptors.

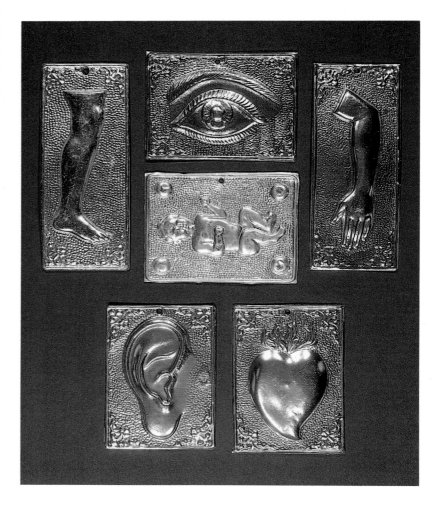

Above left *The Cachuchas*, 1927, shows a group of friends from Kahlo's school days.

Below left Cheap, popular, ex-voto images of parts of the human body, hung by supplicants in religious shrines, were used by Kahlo as jewelry and inspired elements in her own pictures.

Right Frida Kahlo with Diego Rivera, shortly after their first marriage in 1929.

Kahlo played little part in the creation of Rivera's large American murals; instead she accepted the role of dutiful wife – she brought Rivera's lunch to him each day. Her own art developed rapidly, however, even though she only painted a few pictures. *Self-Portrait on the Border between Mexico and the United States* (1932) is perhaps most reflective of her concerns at this time. She shows herself mid-picture, holding a Mexican flag, to her right Detroit, skyscrapered, chimneys belching smoke, all mechanical, electrical and technical. To the left are the ruins, sculpture and artifacts of Mexico's great past civilizations, with a foreground of lush plants and blooms, roots deeply embedded in the ground – an organic contrast. Kahlo's pictorial vocabulary developed to include these above-ground, beneath-ground, inside and outside viewpoints, in which tendrils, connecting threads, roots, and arterial and umbilical-like cords link image to image. Essentially this is a diagrammatic convention of representation, and it has been usual to suggest that she was inspired partly by similar schematic illustrations in her medical textbooks, and partly by Catholic ex-voto pictures, painted in thanksgiving or supplication for divine intervention to aid recovery from some malady or injury.

'MEXICANIDAD' AND KAHLO'S DRESS

Kahlo's wearing of Tehuana dresses, shawls and jewelry dates from 1929, when she married Rivera. It was done apparently at his suggestion, but it conformed with similar efforts by other metropolitan middle-class women to emphasize their Mexican uniqueness by adopting what was perceived as a national

Left Mexican movie star Dolores del Rio, for a while a close friend and lover of Kahlo's.

Right Kahlo and Rivera were feted when they first arrived in New York in 1933, but their visit was curtailed after Rivera refused to delete a figure of Lenin from his Rockefeller Center fresco.

costume. For her first important portrait of 1926, Kahlo had worn a European-style velvet dress. In the same year her father photographed her in a man's suit. During the period 1927-29 her clothes were simple and in keeping with her conscious role as a politically active woman. After her marriage and for the remainder of her life, however, she wore the long embroidered frilled dresses and fringed shawls characteristic of the Tehuantepec region of Mexico, often with necklaces made from fragments of Aztec and Mayan beads. Her earrings and coiled and carefully coiffed hairstyle suggest, and may in part have been inspired by, Pre-Columbian terracotta figures of a type that both she and Rivera collected.

The most mundane reason for adopting this costume was the ability of long skirts to disguise her withered leg. A more sensuous appeal lay in the comfort of such loosely cut clothes. Kahlo's wish publicly to proclaim her Mexican cultural identity has led recent analysts of her life and work to interpret her dress as in some sense an affirmation of female separateness. The Tehuantepec region remains in certain ways a matriarchal subculture, and it has been suggested that Kahlo was especially attracted to its clothing because she knew this. While she undoubtedly did wish to make a point about her cultural heritage, she also made the costume her very own individual uniform. In certain paintings the dress is used as a personal symbol, and in the case of *My Dress Hangs There* (1933) and *Memory* (1937), it is made to stand in as a surrogate figure for Kahlo herself.

Kahlo's depiction of herself in long dresses was also not confined to Tehuantepec or Mexican clothes. In a number of pictures, such as *Frida and Diego Rivera* (1931), her dress is more whimsically archaic than archetypally regional. In *The Two Fridas* (1939), she wears a Victorian lace blouse reminiscent of that worn by her own mother and grandmother, and contrasts

it with a relatively simple, bold Tehuana-style dress. In both paintings her costume is idiosyncratic, combining rustic, populist, old-fashioned, folkish and historical elements – a witty and individual conflation. What is also striking is that Rivera's clothes, by contrast, seem almost deliberately non-Mexican. Kahlo supervised the buying and tailoring of his vast, heavy, three-piece tweed suits. She may also have enjoyed making him a drab foil against which her own plumage would stand out. This would have been utterly in keeping with the Rivera-Kahlo theater of life.

MARRIAGE, MISCARRIAGES, INFIDELITIES, OTHER WOMEN

Kahlo's relationship with Rivera was complex, and in part rooted in their mutual admiration of each other's art. She considered him a genius whose creative magnitude justified a certain waywardness. He became convinced that she was the greatest Mexican artist of her generation. It is doubtful that when Kahlo married Rivera in 1929 she had many illusions about his womanizing. They both lived within a bohemian political circle in which the modish notion of 'free love' was part of the baggage of the politically committed. Kahlo had also already had at least one lesbian affair. Rivera was aware of her

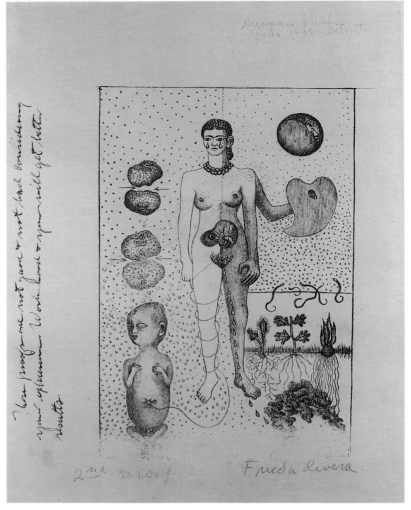

bisexuality when they married, and he later happily sanctioned her taking women as lovers. He already had four children, by three different women, the last of whom, Lupé Marín, was his wife and whom he threw over to marry Kahlo. Rivera's charm, dynamism and success made him extremely attractive to women; he later said that he considered sex as natural as urinating. At their wedding reception Rivera got dead drunk, broke a man's finger and fired off his pistol, and Kahlo temporarily went back to her family. Despite this stormy beginning, the pair settled to a reasonably stable if rather tempestuous life together, much of which, during the first three years, was spent in the United States.

Kahlo's attempts to have Rivera's child have provided the focus for a considerable amount of melodramatic analysis of her life and pictures. Her pregnancy during summer 1932 was certainly a watershed in her life and one about which she has left unusually clear and unambiguous testimony. In one of her most lucidly self-analytical letters, written to a close friend, Dr Leo Eloesser, she makes it evident that initially she wished to abort the child, as she had an earlier one. A local Detroit doctor had given her drugs and castor oil to help her achieve this, but after this proved unsuccessful she decided to carry the baby to term, aided, she hoped, by a Caesarean section that would overcome the problem of her damaged pelvic bones. Kahlo's doubts about bearing a child were motivated by anxiety about hereditary epilepsy in her own family, fear that she might further damage her own fragile health, and Rivera's lack of enthusiasm at the prospect of being a father for the fifth time.

Above left Kahlo's self-portrait lithograph *El Aborto*, 1932, made shortly after her own miscarriage.

Below left Some of Kahlo's imagery was inspired by Pre-Columbian figures such as this.

Above Both Kahlo and Rivera exploited the rather clichéd contrast between white urban culture and the black native tradition. Here Rivera poses movie star Paulette Goddard in May 1940.

In asking Eloesser's advice, Kahlo emphasizes that she has 'the will to do many things' and that she never feels disappointed by life 'as in Russian novels.' The general tone of the letter almost seems to invite her friend to advise her that she should abort. He didn't, but on July 4, three and a half months pregnant, Kahlo lost the child and then spent thirteen awful days in the Henry Ford Hospital, Detroit. She later described the fetus as having simply 'disintegrated' in her womb. Writing after her miscarriage, again to Eloesser, she explained her wish to have a child as 'rather a biological thing' and wrote that, while unhappy, she felt that 'now that it has happened there is nothing to do but put up with it.' This did not, however, prevent her from making art from her misfortune.

Kahlo's gruesome picture, *Henry Ford Hospital* (1932), was provoked by the miscarriage, and shows her lying naked on a blood-stained sheet while around her float a fetus, a snail, a sterilizer, a purple flower, a pelvis, and a plastercast of a woman's lower torso of the type used to teach medical students. A similar diagrammatic approach is seen in the lithograph *Miscarriage* or *El Aborto*, done in Detroit at the same time. A few months after her miscarriage, Kahlo's mother died, an event that

stimulated her to paint *My Birth* (1932), in which the head of herself as a newborn child emerges from between the legs of a woman. This trio of pictures, along with another entitled *Frida and the Caesarian Operation*, are possibly the first twentieth-century fine art pictures of childbirth – certainly nothing as graphically explicit is found in European art of the period.

Comparisons have often been drawn between these pictures and ancient Mexican, Polynesian and Indian statues. *My Birth* may in fact have been directly inspired by an Aztec sculpture of the goddess Tlazolteolt. During the 1970s, when feminist cultural critics and artists began to claim space for a specifically female subject-matter, in which menstruation, childbirth and pain figured largely, Kahlo's pictures in general, and these three pictures in particular, were embraced as inspirational antecedents. That they may have been connected with even earlier ancient images was viewed as compounding their significance, suggesting that Kahlo might in some proto-feminist way have viewed the world's history as one in which archetypes of life and female potency were paramount.

The symbolism employed in the *Henry Ford Hospital* painting, as with her earlier portrait on the Mexican border, again contrasts the mechanical and unpleasant (sterilizer and pelvis cast) with the soft and organic. The snail is intended to evoke the physical feeling of the miscarriage, while the flower is supposed to be more generally suggestive of genitalia and Kahlo's own eroticism.

Despite these dreadful events, and the art that flowed from them, it is by no means clear that Kahlo herself was in the longer term so concerned with having a child. She subsequently obtained a fetus in a bottle of formaldehyde, which she kept on a shelf in her home and would shock visitors by telling them that it was her own still-born child. Kahlo's famous levity and black sense of humor is sometimes ignored in discussions of her suffering. While she may have had a morbid obsession with childbirth, which surfaced in her art and conversation throughout her life, as she said herself, she had much else to preoccupy her.

Serious differences between Kahlo and Rivera first arose only after December 1933. Rivera enjoyed the adulation, money and notoriety of his four years in the United States and was resentful at having to return to Mexico. Kahlo was homesick and glad to be back. Crisis came when Rivera's philandering extended to a long affair with Cristina, Kahlo's sister. The painting *A Few Small Nips* (1935) is usually regarded as directly symbolic of Kahlo's unhappiness at this time. A man stands over the bloody knife-slashed corpse of his naked lover. The picture illustrated a current newspaper story in which an arrested murderer pleaded that he had used only 'a few little pricks' to chastise his woman. Following her discovery of Rivera's affair, Kahlo left home, took an apartment in central Mexico City, and later went to New York. When the affair with Cristina ended Kahlo returned to Rivera, but she also took several lovers of her own, and a kind of understanding developed between herself and Rivera. She tolerated his infidelities and infatuations, even discussing aspects of the affairs with him; he, on the other hand, was kept in the dark about her own

liaisons. Despite this it seems clear that, however much she may have joked about Rivera's conduct, she would have preferred it to be otherwise.

Despite her operations, bed-bound convalescences and pain, Kahlo, according to the available accounts of some of her ex-lovers, led a remarkably active sex-life. It was her affair with Trotsky in 1937, while he and his wife were staying with herself and Rivera, that may have led Rivera to sue for divorce. The couple separated in November, 1938, only to remarry thirteen months later. During the interim Kahlo was devastated, she drank heavily, had psychiatric treatment and her health deteriorated. Rivera was persuaded by Dr Eloesser, their mutual Californian friend, to return to her and remarry.

A number of paintings touch directly upon events during this most serious estrangement between Kahlo and Rivera. *Two Nudes in the Jungle* (1939), a picture that she gave to Dolores del Rio, suggests Kahlo's bisexuality, with its naked white-skinned woman resting her head on the lap of a brown-skinned woman. From the undergrowth the women are watched by a monkey – traditional symbol of sin, the devil and animal sexuality. *The Two Fridas* (1939) shows two sides of Kahlo's personality, one with a bleeding heart in antiquated European dress, the other in Tehuana costume, holding a locket showing Rivera as a small boy. The meaning is unclear, although Kahlo seems for once to be giving emphasis to her non-Mexican attributes, the side that Rivera apparently did not like. It may simply be that the European element represents Rivera's jealousy of her success – her affair with Trotsky, her

Left Trotsky and his wife greeted by Kahlo on arrival in Mexico in 1937. Kahlo later took him as a lover, and was for a while suspected of complicity in his murder.

Right Kahlo's pet monkeys appear in several of her paintings, usually as a traditional symbol of sexual liberation.

developing independent reputation, and her friendship with various Americans, not least with the photographer Nickolas Muray, who became her lover, and who was responsible for some of the most exquisite photographs of her both in black and white and color.

KAHLO AND SURREALISM

In a Surrealist map of the world published in the Belgian magazine *Varieties* in 1929, Mexico's border is shown abutting Labrador and Alaska, with the United States completely missing. Mexico enjoyed a special position in this highly selective and idealized Surrealist world, along with the Easter Islands, Constantinople, and Peru – places perceived as exotic, primitive and mysterious, and preferred over countries whose traditions of art and literature were Western and Christian. André Breton, the Surrealist leader, was one of the strongest of the Mexican enthusiasts and he collected Pre-Columbian sculpture. Breton first visited Mexico in April 1938 and became part of the circle of artists and writers which included Kahlo, Rivera and Trotsky. He enthused over Kahlo's

work and later that year wrote a preface for the catalog of an exhibition of her pictures held at the Julien Levy Gallery in New York. He described her art as 'pure surreality' and rather patronizingly suggested that this was 'despite the fact that it had been conceived without any prior knowledge whatsoever of the ideas motivating the activities of my friends and myself.' Kahlo's laconic response, printed in the gallery's press release, was: 'I never knew I was a Surrealist until André Breton came to Mexico and told me I was one. I myself don't know what I am.' The exhibition, held in a gallery that was especially associated with Surrealist art, represented Kahlo's first major public exposure. She sold well, was reviewed with enthusiasm, and the future looked promising.

Kahlo's pictures certainly do *look* surrealist. Her strange floating forms, interior and exterior viewpoints, exaggerated and disparate scales of objects, have a visual kinship with paintings by Dali or Magritte. But whereas much Surrealist art is concerned with associations leading to new meanings, with the metamorphosis of objects into something strange and novel, much of Kahlo's symbolism is more straightforwardly intelligible, usually representing specific autobiographical problems or anxieties. Only in the small number of later pictures from the 1940s of flowers and foliage metamorphosed into wombs, fallopian tubes and penises does she seem to be pursuing something more purely surreal; mostly her images, however bizarre, remain emblematic.

On the back of one of her 1944 drawings, Kahlo wrote: 'Surrealism is the magical surprise of finding a lion in a wardrobe when you were sure of finding shirts,' a definition of Surrealism not dissimilar from the more famous designation of it by the poet Lautréamont as 'the chance meeting of a sewing machine and an umbrella on a dissection table.' The question that remains, however, is how far Kahlo chose to paint the way she did knowing that it would or could be bracketed with Surrealism. In one interview she accepted that she was a Surrealist but suggested that her Surrealism was essentially capricious and humorous, a point that had been emphasized earlier by the critic Bertram Wolfe, writing for *Vogue* about her New York show:

While official Surrealism concerns itself with the stuff of dreams, nightmares and neurotic symbols, in Madame Rivera's brand of it wit and humor predominates.

Despite reservations, Kahlo accepted André Breton's invitation to visit Paris in January 1939, where he helped organize a display of 17 of her pictures as the centerpiece of an exhibition entitled 'Mexique' at the Pierre Colle Gallery. Poor organization, cramped conditions in the Breton's flat, food poisoning and a kidney infection which Kahlo blamed on the Breton's lack of hygiene, and Breton's borrowing money from her, all led Kahlo to have a very poor view of the Parisian Surrealist circle. Although her exhibition was successful – the Louvre bought one of her paintings and Picasso and Kandinsky both praised her work – Kahlo left Europe 'nauseated' by what she described as the degeneracy of democracies that were 'not worth a crumb' and the 'damn intellectual' posturing of left-bank Paris café society. In one letter she wrote:

I rather [sic] sit on the floor in the market of Toluca and sell tortillas than to have anything to do with those 'artistic' bitches of Paris. They sit for hours in the 'cafés' warming their precious behinds, and talk for hours without stopping about 'culture,' 'art,' 'revolution' and so on and so forth . . . poisoning the air with theories. It was worthwhile to come here only to see why Europe is rotting, why all these people [sic] – good for nothing – are the cause of all the Hitlers and Mussolinis.

Kahlo's forthright and clichéd anti-intellectualism echoed the prejudices she had earlier formed about the United States. While in Paris she had helped evacuate 400 Spanish anti-Franco refugees to Mexico. Such straightforward action to aid fellow left-wing victims of war appealed to her more than debate. Later, around 1952, Kahlo wrote: 'I detest Surrealism, to me it seems a decadent manifestation of bourgeois art.' By then, of course, Surrealism was no longer fashionable. It does appear on balance that Kahlo exploited the popularity, the craze, for Surrealism and was prepared, however briefly, to use

associations made between her own art and that of the group. She exhibited in a number of Surrealist group shows throughout the 1940s and was certainly linked with Surrealism in the public mind. Not the least part of Kahlo's appeal to the European Surrealists was Kahlo herself, dressed in her fantastic costume, which caused a minor sensation both in New York and in Paris. It is ironic that, while to the Surrealists Kahlo represented an exotic alternative to Western values, she came to see Surrealism as symptomatic of the inherent corruption of those same values.

LAUGHING AT DEATH

I drink to drown my sorrows, but the damn things have learned to swim.

The first thing Kahlo saw each morning when she awoke was a skeleton. Fixed to the underside of the canopy of her narrow four-poster bed was a full-scale *papier-mâché* figure – her 'lover' was how Rivera jokingly described this giant bony doll of the type traditionally used in Mexico's famous November All Souls 'Day of the Dead' celebrations. Carried through the crowded streets and festooned in firecrackers, such exploding figures terrified and delighted festive crowds, who dissipated their anxieties about death and fear of dying by laughing and embracing the figures as companions in life. Three of Kahlo's pictures, *Four Inhabitants of Mexico City* (1938), *The Wounded Table* (1940), and *The Dream* (1940), all celebrate this popular skeleton.

Below left The beautiful journalist
Dorothy Hale, whose suicide in
1938 prompted one of Kahlo's most
gruesome pictures.

Right Kahlo, wearing a Pre-
Columbian bead necklace and
Tehuantapec dress, applies with
Rivera for the licence for their
second marriage in 1940.

Kahlo's attitude to death, grounded in Mexican popular Catholic culture, and laced with her own taste for the gothically shocking, could sometimes unsettle American purchasers, who were more respectful of mortality's attendant social obligations. For example her picture *The Suicide of Dorothy Hale* (1939) made the commissioning patron 'physically sick.' Clare Boothe Luce, editor of *Vogue*, thought she would be getting a head and shoulders portrait of Dorothy Hale, suitable to give the dead woman's mother: instead she got an ex-voto that graphically showed the burst body of her friend on the sidewalk beneath her New York apartment. Kahlo had been told the story at her New York 1938 exhibition opening – of how the beautiful, talented, widowed, jilted ex-journalist Dorothy Hale had held a cocktail party to celebrate her 'departure' and then after midnight had thrown herself to her death. She had even carefully selected her frock and corsage of yellow roses before she jumped, fastidious attention to detail that would have appealed to a meticulous dresser like Kahlo.

The painting as it now survives is altered. Clare Booth Luce was persuaded not to destroy it but she had painted out an upper inscription, 'The Suicide of Dorothy Hale painted at the request of Clare Booth Luce for the mother of Dorothy.' 'I wouldn't have requested such a gory picture for my worst enemy, much less my unfortunate friend,' were her final words on this distasteful subject. It has been suggested that Kahlo's sympathy for the loneliness and despair of Dorothy Hale makes this picture into a more general indictment of women driven to despair by male desertion (Kahlo and Rivera were separated when she painted it), but it was surely the dramatic perfection of the gesture that attracted Kahlo. Her ghoulish, almost child-like, elaboration of the blood stain underlining the word

'suicide' on the picture's inscription suggests a concentrated absorption with the grim artistry of the work that spared little feeling for either victim or viewer. Indeed Kahlo may have wished to confront an urbane, and to her mind effete, viewer with the rebarbative but more direct honesty of her own culture's popular iconography. One is reminded of the great New York photo-journalist 'WeeGee,' at his peak during this period, who himself was not above artistically re-arranging a corpse on a sidewalk to achieve maximum front-page shock.

Kahlo's earlier painting, *The Deceased Dimas* (1937), also a corpse portrait, is of a poor three-year-old Indian boy who was Rivera's godchild and had also been his model. Laid out on a straw mat, dressed like a little mitered bishop with a gladiolus flower as crozier, Dimas is an *angelito*, baptised, without sin, guaranteed a place in heaven where he may intercede for his earthbound parents and family. Portraits and photographs of such 'saints' were popular. Had it been possible in Mexico, as in Palermo in Sicily, for ordinary people to preserve the actual body of the dead, no doubt it would have been done. Instead these macabre portraits record the beloved in death rather than showing them happily alive, the last-moment immediacy of departure preferred over more pleasant memories. Kahlo's addition of a Frankenstein-like dribble of blood from the mouth of Dimas, however, and his half-open eyes, take this portrait beyond the realm of pious funereal record and turn it into something more knowing, closer to a condescending black joke at the expense of ignorant believers. Kahlo's own anti-Catholicism perhaps made it difficult for her not to mock while she was painting in this folk-genre. On other occasions, when she used the grandiose iconography of ancient Pre-Columbian Mexico beliefs, she was never less than reverential.

DECLINE

The last decade of Kahlo's life with Rivera was less tempestuous. He continued to be unfaithful but they did evolve a calmer home life. Kahlo's artistic horizons expanded too, and following her success in New York and Paris she was elected in 1942 to the Seminario de Cultura Mexicana, a body that was broadly responsible for the promotion of Mexican culture. In the following years she was appointed by the Ministry of Public Education to teach a group of students in a newly-formed national School of Painting and Sculpture. Until ill-health prevented her discharging this duty, she ran a successful class, characterized by a hands-off approach that encouraged students

Above The young Kahlo and Rivera were both included in Rivera's 1948 mural for the Hotel del Prado, Mexico City.

Right Kahlo's bedroom with her narrow bed, at the foot of which is her framed group of Marxist heroes.

to develop their own talents without the constraint of more formal instruction.

Rivera came to play an increasingly important part in her art. They had always shared a proclivity to generate fantasies around their life together: there had always been a considerable amount of childlike play together. She, for example, bought him rubber ducks to play with in the bath; he augmented her collection of dolls. But now Rivera himself appears as a child in her pictures. Whereas in 1937 Kahlo had depicted herself as an infant suckled by a mighty female Pre-Columbian figure (*My Nurse*), in 1949 in *The Love Embrace of the Universe, the Earth (Mexico), Diego, Me, and Senor Xolotl*, it is she who actually cradles giant baby Rivera. In her diary she wrote:

> Diego, beginning
> Diego, constructor
> Diego, my child
> Diego, my bridegroom
> Diego, painter
> Diego, my lover
> Diego, my husband
> Diego, my friend
> Diego, my father
> Diego, my mother
> Diego, my son
> Diego, I
> Diego, Universe
> diversity in Unity.

Kahlo's health began seriously to decline from about 1944. In addition to damage from her accident and subsequent operations, she was an alcoholic, and had probably already established, or was well on the way to establishing, her addiction to pain-killing drugs. She became increasingly dependent upon Rivera and her periods of bed-bound convalescence grew more protracted. In 1951 she had a series of operations upon her spine. Poor circulation led in 1953 to her right leg being amputated below the knee. In her later years Kahlo kept a diary, which provides an invaluable insight into her anxieties and panic as she felt herself slipping closer to death. She contemplated suicide, but jokingly stated that it was impossible because Rivera would miss her. In early 1953 she had her final public exhibition, the first solo show of her work in Mexico. She was too ill to attend but had herself taken to the gallery in an ambulance. At the private view she lay on a bed in the center of the gallery surrounded by guests.

The last public appearance that Kahlo made was on July 2, 1954, at a peace rally protesting against the CIA destabilization of the democratically elected government of Guatemala.

Eleven days later she died. After the public lying-in-state of her body at the Palace of Fine Arts in Mexico City, her coffin was carried out draped with a hammer and sickle flag. Rivera's refusal to remove this flag apparently helped gain him readmission to the Mexican Communist Party. Kahlo in her last years had grown closer to the party and from the late 1940s she and Rivera became much more heavily involved in active left-wing politics. Rivera had to atone for his friendship with Trotsky, his opposition to Stalin during the war, and his anarchic anti-centralist views. Kahlo, having never been expelled from the party, had merely to prove that she did not necessarily share Rivera's views.

In 1951 she wrote that she felt that her paintings up to then had been an expression of herself, but now she wanted them to serve the party and 'the Revolution.' Having denounced Surrealism, she distanced herself from Rivera by arguing that she was a better Communist, and claimed that she had only agreed to have Trotsky in their home at Rivera's insistence. Rivera meanwhile was painting two enormous expiatory canvases entitled *The Nightmare of War and the Dream of Peace* and *Glorious Victory*, denouncing United States and Western engagement in the Korean War. Refused exhibition in Mexico, these were shown in Paris with the assistance of the French Communist Party and later in China. Despite her stated change of direction, Kahlo's own more political pictures continued to use the same symbolic conventions that she had employed all her life.

It was not until her last year and the painting of her two final pictures that she became crudely instructional. The first, *Marxism Will Give Health to the Sick* (1954), shows the head of Marx hovering like a protective sub-deity behind a large pair of hands that enclose the broken and corseted body of Kahlo. Another hand throttles a caricatured Uncle Sam. The dove of peace flies above a globe on which the red of the Soviet map extends. The second, *Frida and Stalin* (1954), shows Kahlo sitting before a huge portrait of the recently deceased dictator. Both pictures are an embarrassment to devotees of the Kahlo legend and to those who revere her art, and it has been usual to suggest that they were an aberration brought on in part by a craving for some reassuring universal system of belief, and in part by her drug-induced debility. Although they may be dismissed as pitiable, they also represent a sad nemesis, a reflection of Kahlo's propensity for hero-worship, of the Mexican Revolution, and of Rivera himself, now elided into adulation for an apparently paternal leader of international Communism. In her final pictures the world is presented as simplistically polarized into goodies and baddies.

Left Kahlo shortly before her death in 1954.

Right Kahlo's coffin lying in state, draped with the Communist flag, at the Palace of Fine Arts, Mexico City.

SELF-PORTRAITS

Kahlo does not perceptibly age over two decades of self-portraits. Her 1920s visage is youthful and varied; her 1931 double portrait with Rivera shows her curiously doll-like; but by 1933 she had settled to a facial formula from which she deviated little. Kahlo was much photographed, most famously by Imogen Cunningham around 1930, later in color by her lover Nickolas Muray in 1938. Comparing photographs with self-portraits reveals how she manipulated her own image, thickening and adding emphasis to the arch of her eyebrows, making them meet in the dense bush above the bridge of her nose, giving herself a fuller, slightly shorter mouth, and delineating hair by hair the downy moustache on her upper lip.

In Catholic cultures female hair has always connoted the dangerous territory of active sex: cut off or completely covered by nuns, worn under a hat or veil by churchgoers, long tresses are the traditional badge of the Magdalen. Kahlo's elaborate coiffure and exaggeration of her own facial hair are part of the projection of her own erotic forwardness. Several portraits show her accompanied by monkeys, ancient symbols of lust; others include parrots, in Hindu mythology the bearers of the love god Kama. When Kahlo wished to show herself 'un-sexed' by the trauma of her divorce in 1939, she painted herself shorn and wearing a man's suit. When she wished to celebrate reconciliation a year later, her hair is shown prominently standing up in a double figure-of-eight like a giant Staffordshire knot.

The background to several of the head-and-shoulders self-portraits of the 1940s is a forest of huge leaves, cacti and flowers, insistently fecund and fertile. An important variation in these head-and-shoulder pictures involves the substitution of Kahlo's distinctive Pre-Columbian necklaces for entwining thorns that pierce her neck and draw forth precise, minute beads of blood – never, however, with any apparent effect upon her composure. Kahlo doesn't wince, doesn't smile; she often cries tears, but these always appear as added glycerine droplets, which emblematically suggest, rather than truly document, pain. The mask remains unchanging. Only in the picture actually entitled *The Mask* (1945), where Kahlo holds up a truly contorted and painful weeping mask in front of her face, do we see real pain.

Precedents for Kahlo's head-and-shoulders self-portrait practice are not easy to find among artists who have turned to their own face for inspiration. Rembrandt's self-portraits are more empirical, chronicling his changing face and fortune; Van Gogh's are slightly closer in spirit, prompted as several were by dramatic events in the artist's life; but the most suggestive pedigree is the art of Dante Gabriel Rossetti, where the repetitive, the symbolic and the sexual can be found in his several images of women made from about 1860 onward. It may seem strange to invoke Rossetti, who has been vilified by feminist cultural historians, in order to illuminate Kahlo, but there is an extent to which she too aestheticizes her face in order to remove it from record and render it iconic.

One may also draw parallels between the format Kahlo adopts and small Italian and Northern European Madonna and Child votive images, especially those that are loaded with goldfinches, lilies, pomegranates, cherries, lemons, and the other flora and fauna traditionally symbolic of Mary or the Christ Child's future suffering. Rossetti also drew upon these earlier religious images and the associations that they inevitably provoked in the spectator's mind. Although there is a sense in which virtually all Kahlo's pictures are 'self' portraits, it is appropriate to isolate these head-and-shoulders paintings for separate consideration. When she shows herself full length there is often a much clearer narrative, a more specific biographical exposition. In, for example, *The Broken Column* (1944), *Tree of Hope* (1946), or *Without Hope* (1946), we see her presented as an actress in her own distressing medical drama. In the earlier *Self-Portrait On the Border* (1932) and *The Two Fridas* (1939), she hovers between two cultures, with some choice and some action implicit, but in the head-and-shoulders pictures, stiffness and a certain glacial distance is usual and her self-presentation is altogether more ethereal.

ABOVE
Portrait of Alicia Galant, 1927
Oil on canvas, 38¼ × 33 inches (97 × 84 cm)
Collection of the Dolores Olmedo Foundation, Mexico City

RIGHT
Portrait of Miguel N. Lira, 1927
Oil on canvas, 42⅛ × 38⅞ inches (107 × 93.5 cm)
Instituto Tlaxcalteca de Cultura, Tlaxcala, Mexico

Portrait of Cristina, 1928
Oil on panel, 31⅛ × 23⅝ inches (79 × 60 cm)
Sotheby's, New York, NY

Portrait of Virginia (Niña), 1929
Oil on masonite, 30¼ × 23¾ inches (77 × 60 cm)
Collection of the Dolores Olmedo Foundation, Mexico City

29

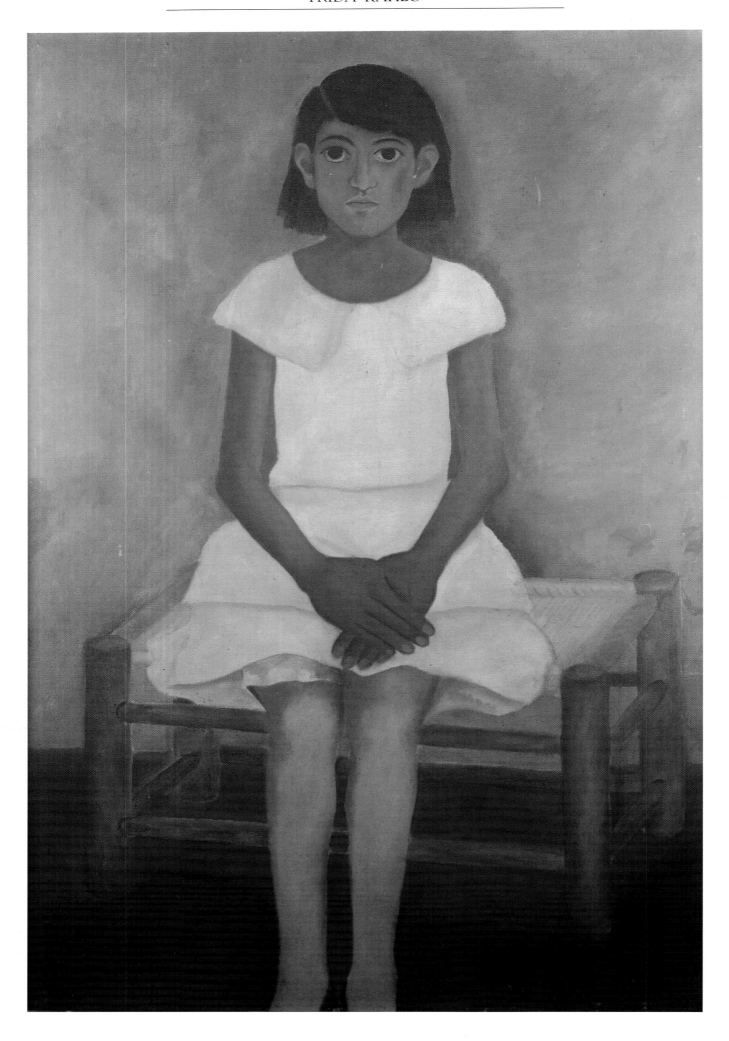

ABOVE

Portrait of a Girl, 1929
Oil on canvas, 46½ × 31½ inches (118 × 80 cm)
Collection of the Frida Kahlo Museum, Mexico City

RIGHT

Dos Mujeres (Two Women), 1929
Oil on canvas, 27⅜ × 21 inches (69.6 × 53.3 cm)
Mary-Anne Martin/Fine Art, New York, NY

Self-Portrait, 1930
Oil on canvas, 25½ × 21⅛ inches (64.8 × 53.7 cm)
Anonymous loan
Courtesy, Museum of Fine Arts, Boston, MA

Portrait of Lady Cristina Hastings, 1931
Pencil on paper, 19 × 12¼ inches (48.3 × 31.1 cm)
Collection of the Dolores Olmedo Foundation, Mexico City

Frida Kahlo -31
"Retrato de Lady Hastings".
San Francisco. Cal.

ABOVE

Portrait of Luther Burbank, 1931
Oil on canvas masonite, 33½ × 24 inches
(85 × 61 cm)
Collection of the Dolores Olmedo Foundation, Mexico City

RIGHT

Portrait of Dr Leo Eloesser, 1931
Oil on masonite, 33½ × 23½ inches (85 × 59.7 cm)
Collection of the University of California
School of Medicine, San Francisco, CA

ABOVE

Portrait of Eva Frederick, 1931

Oil on canvas, 24½ × 17¾ inches (62 × 45 cm)

Collection of the Dolores Olmedo Foundation, Mexico City

Frida and Diego Rivera, 1931

Oil on canvas, 39⅜ × 31 inches (100.01 × 78.75 cm)

Gift of Albert M. Bender, Albert M. Bender Collection

San Francisco Museum of Modern Art, CA (36.6061)

Henry Ford Hospital, 1932
Oil on metal, 12 × 15 inches (30.5 × 38 cm)
Collection of the Dolores Olmedo Foundation, Mexico City

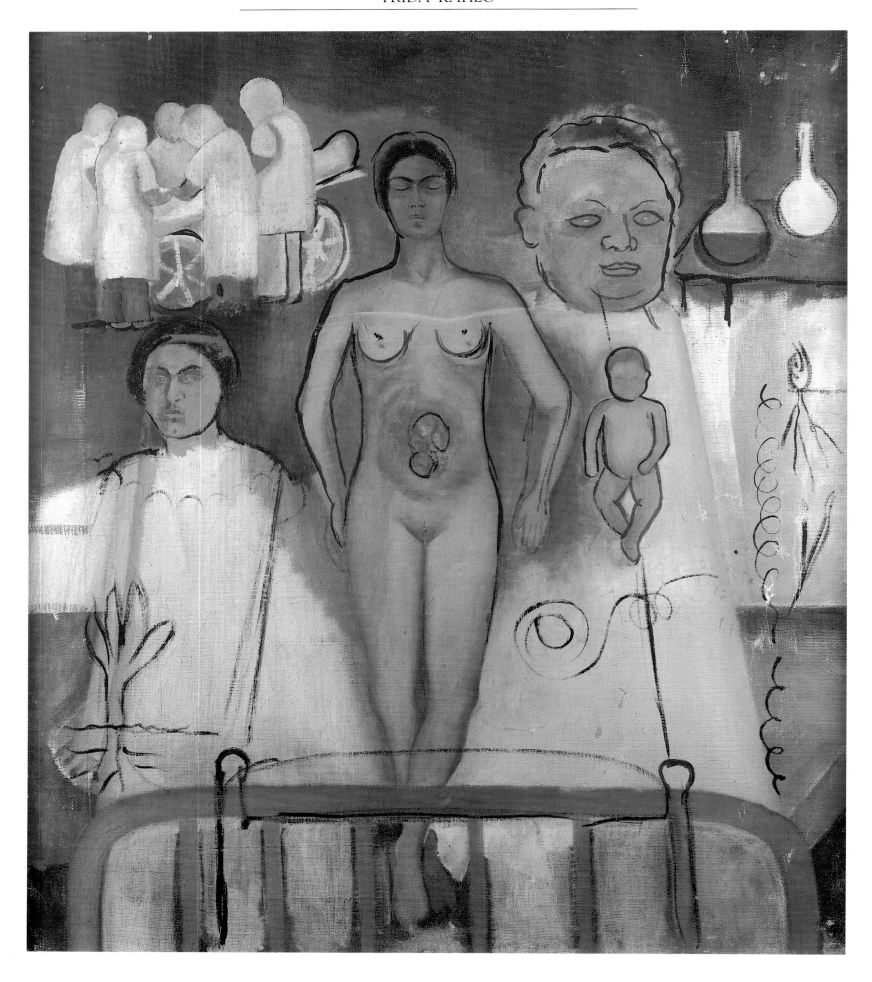

Frida and the Caesarian Operation, c.1932
Oil on canvas, 28¾ × 24½ inches (73 × 62.2 cm)
Collection of the Frida Kahlo Museum, Mexico City

Self-Portrait, 'Very Ugly', 1933
Fresco panel, 27¼ × 22¼ inches (69.2 × 57.2 cm)
Private Collection
Photo courtesy of Dr Salomon Grimberg

ABOVE
Self-Portrait Dedicated to Leon Trotsky, 1937
Oil on masonite, 30 × 24 inches (76.2 × 60.1 cm)
Gift of the Honorable Clare Booth Luce
National Museum of Women in the Arts,
Washington, D.C.

LEFT
The Deceased Dimas, 1937
Oil on masonite, 18⅞ × 12⅜ inches (48 × 31.5 cm)
Collection of the Dolores Olmedo Foundation, Mexico City

ABOVE
Portrait of Diego Rivera, 1937
Oil on masonite, 18⅛ × 12½ inches (46 × 31.2 cm)
Jacques and Natasha Gelman Collection, Mexico

RIGHT
Self-Portrait: The Frame, 1938
Oil on aluminum and glass, 18⅞ × 12⅜ inches
(48 × 31.5 cm)
Musée National d'Art Moderne, Paris

LEFT

Itzcuintli Dog with Me, 1938

Oil on canvas, 29½ × 21¾ inches (74.9 × 55.2 cm)

Private Collection

Photograph courtesy of the National Museum of Women in
the Arts, Washington, D.C.

ABOVE

Self-Portrait with Monkey, 1938

Oil on masonite, 16 × 12 inches (40.1 × 30 cm)

Bequest of A. Conger Goodyear, 1966

Albright-Knox Art Gallery, Buffalo, NY (66:9:10)

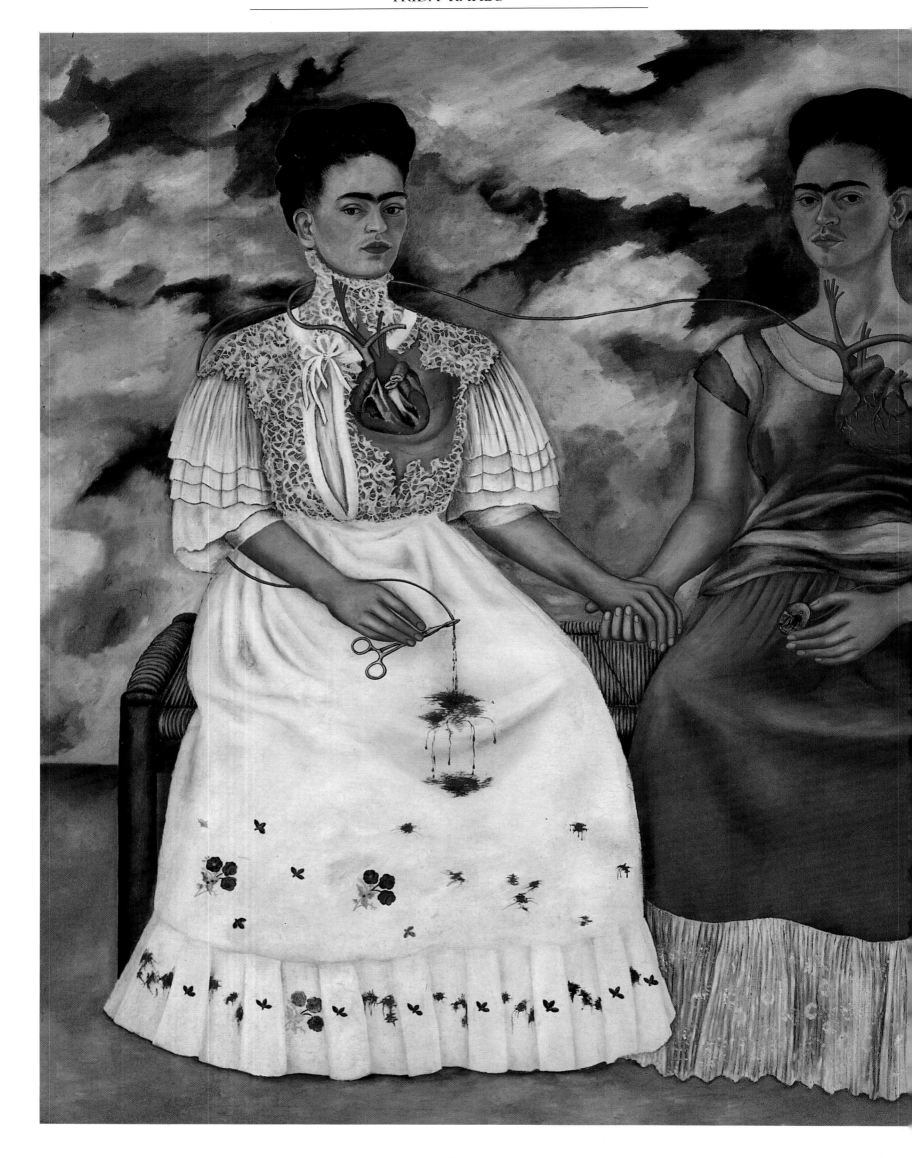

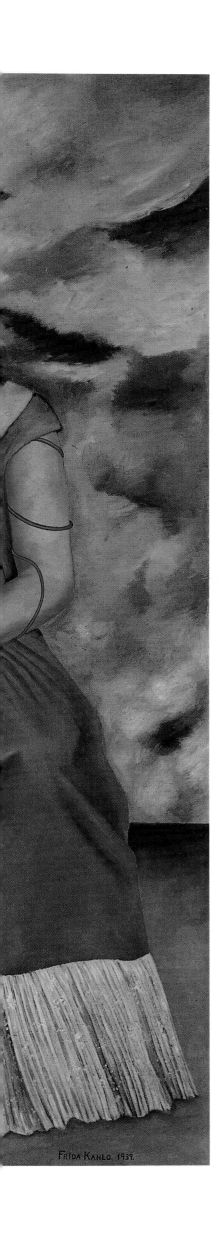

The Two Fridas, 1939
Oil on canvas, 67 × 67 inches (170 × 170 cm)
Collection of the Museo de Arte Moderno, Mexico City

Retrato de Mrs Jean Wight
pintado en Enero de 1931, en la ciudad
de San Francisco Cal. por Frieda Kahlo.

Self-Portrait with Thorn Necklace and Hummingbird, 1940
Oil on canvas, 24¼ × 17¾ inches (61.6 × 45 cm)
Harry Ransom Humanities Research Center Art Collection
University of Texas, Austin, TX (66.6)

LEFT
Portrait of Mrs Jean Wight, 1931
Oil on canvas, 24⅞ × 18⅛ inches (63.2 × 46 cm)
Berggruen Gallery, San Francisco, CA

Pinté mi retrato en el año de 1940
para el Doctor Leo Eloesser, mi médico y
mi mejor amigo. Con todo mi cariño. Frida Kahlo—

Self-Portrait, 1940
Oil on masonite, 23½ × 15¾ inches (59.7 × 40 cm)
Mary-Anne Martin/Fine Art, New York, NY

Self-Portrait with Braid, 1941
Oil on masonite, 20 × 15¼ inches (51 × 38.7 cm)
Jacques and Natasha Gelman Collection, Mexico

Self-Portrait with Monkey and Parrot, 1942
Oil on hardboard, 20⅞ × 17 inches (53.3 × 43.2 cm)
Photo courtesy IBM Corporation Archive, Armonk, NY

Thinking About Death, 1943
Oil on canvas mounted on masonite, 17¾ × 14½ inches
(45 × 36.8 cm)
Private Collection
Photograph courtesy of Dr Salomon Grimberg

ABOVE
Diego in my Thoughts, 1943
Oil on masonite, 30 × 24 inches (76 × 61 cm)
Jacques and Natasha Gelman Collection, Mexico

RIGHT
Self-Portrait with Monkeys, 1943
Oil on canvas, 32 × 24¾ inches (81.5 × 63 cm)
Jacques and Natasha Gelman Collection, Mexico

Portrait of Natasha Gelman, 1943
Oil on masonite, 11¾ × 9 inches (30 × 23 cm)
Jacques and Natasha Gelman Collection, Mexico

The Broken Column, 1944
Oil on masonite, 15¾ × 12¼ inches (40 × 31 cm)
Collection of the Dolores Olmedo Foundation, Mexico City

RIGHT
Dona Rosita Morillo, 1944
Oil on canvas mounted on masonite, 29¾ × 23½ inches
(75.5 × 59.5 cm)
Collection of the Dolores Olmedo Foundation, Mexico City

ABOVE
Portrait of the Engineer Edwardo Morillo Zafa, 1944
Oil on masonite, 15½ × 11½ inches (39.5 × 29.2 cm)
Collection of the Dolores Olmedo Foundation, Mexico City

RIGHT
Dona Rosita Morillo, 1944
Oil on canvas mounted on masonite, 29¾ × 23½ inches
(75.5 × 59.5 cm)
Collection of the Dolores Olmedo Foundation, Mexico City

ABOVE

Portrait of Lupito Morillo Zafa, 1944

Oil on hardboard, 22½ × 19⅝ inches (57 × 50 cm)

Private Collection

Courtesy CDS Gallery, USA, Galeria Arvil, Mexico

RIGHT

Self-Portrait with Small Monkey, 1945

Oil on masonite, 22 × 15¾ inches (55 × 40 cm)

Collection of the Dolores Olmedo Foundation, Mexico City

ABOVE

The Mask, 1945

Oil on canvas, 15¾ × 12¼ inches (40 × 31 cm)

Collection of the Dolores Olmedo Foundation, Mexico City

RIGHT

Tree of Hope, 1946

Oil on masonite, 22 × 16 inches (55.9 × 40 cm)

Collection of Isidore Ducasse Fine Arts, New York, NY

Without Hope, 1945
Oil on canvas mounted on masonite,
11 × 14¼ inches (28 × 36 cm)
Collection of the Dolores Olmedo Foundation,
Mexico City

ABOVE

Self-Portrait with Loose Hair, 1947

Oil on masonite, 24 × 17¾ inches (61.5 × 45.5 cm)

Mary-Anne Martin/Fine Art, New York, NY

RIGHT

Diego and I, 1949

Oil on masonite, 11⅝ × 8¹³⁄₁₆ inches (29.5 × 22.3 cm)

Mary-Anne Martin/Fine Art, New York, NY

RIGHT
Self-Portrait with the Image of Diego on my Breast and Maria on My Brow, 1953/54
Oil on masonite, 24 × 16 inches (61 × 41 cm)
Private Collection
Photograph courtesy of Dr Salomon Grimberg

ABOVE
Portrait of My Father, Wilhelm Kahlo, 1951
Oil on masonite, 24½ × 19 inches (62.2 × 48.2 cm)
Collection of the Frida Kahlo Museum, Mexico City

STILL LIFE

Rivera's characteristic painting surface was a hundred square feet or more of wall, his pictorial content some sweeping, didactic, socially critical essay on conflicts between rich and poor. Kahlo's more usual support was tinplate, masonite, or canvas mounted on masonite, her scale invariably small. She seems to have deliberately avoided essays in the grand manner and to have been content with a more microcosmic focus, perhaps never more so than in her still-lifes.

Kahlo's decision to paint small still-life pictures, like that which governed her increased output of smaller self-portraits after about 1940, may in part have been influenced by her wish to gain greater financial independence from Rivera. Both types of picture were relatively uncomplicated and, judging from the number now in private collections, more easily marketable. The type of still life that Kahlo painted – close-ups of cut segments of watermelon and other exotic Central American fruit and vegetables – was a well-established, rather old-fashioned genre of Mexican painting and by the 1940s had slightly whimsical associations.

What Kahlo brought to the genre was a robust, and at times extremely forthright, overlay of sexual suggestiveness. Her allegory is never complex and her emblems are usually straightforward, for example, the inclusion of a parrot to represent sex, or the addition of a dove symbolic of peace. What is most striking, however, is the actual shapes of the fruit depicted: split open to reveal seeds or round, protuberant and ruddy, evocative of female genitalia; bananas and mushrooms, phallic in shape. This biomorphic allusiveness was a well-established part of Surrealist pictorial strategies, employed by among others Dali and Tanguy, and was intended to unnerve spectators, to confront them with objects of hyper-real intensity that uncomfortably brought to the surface suppressed or subconscious sexual urgings. There is no doubt that this was Kahlo's intention, and the best of these pictures are among the wittiest of all her works.

Only toward the very end of Kahlo's life do her still-life pictures perceptibly shift their meaning, losing their sexual resonance and becoming more directly evocative of nature itself. Kahlo sometimes became so ill after 1951 that she was unable to paint anything other than little pictures of the fruits that lay by her bedside. Despite her physical weakness, she tried to make these small works carry more weighty significance than the purely observational. Tendrils and roots are at times made to spell out words like 'Life' and she reverted to putting in the sun and moon in the background, with night-time and day-time skies. These pictures, painted after she had made the decision to take a more political direction, show her clearly diminished powers. Her attempts to extend allegorical meaning resulted in these pictures falling short of the clarity of the best still-lifes of the 1940s.

RIGHT
Still Life, 1925
Oil on canvas mounted on board,
16¼ × 12 inches (41.2 × 30 cm)
Sotheby's, New York, NY

LEFT
Still Life: "Life, How I Love You," 1938
Oil on board, 22 × 14 inches (55.6 × 35.6 cm)
Private Collection
Photograph courtesy of Dr Salomon Grimberg

ABOVE
Still Life: Pitahayas, 1938
Oil on aluminum, 10 × 14 inches (25.4 × 35.6 cm)
Bequest of Rudolph and Louise Langer
Collection of the Madison Art Center, Madison, WI

Still Life with Prickly Pear Fruit, 1938
Oil on tin, 7⅞ × 9⅞ inches (19.9 × 25 cm)
Mary-Anne Martin/Fine Art, New York, NY

Flower Basket, 1941
Oil on copper, diameter 25½ inches (64.7 cm)
Mary-Anne Martin/Fine Art, New York, NY

The Bride Frightened at Seeing Life Opened, 1943
Oil on canvas, 23¾ × 32 inches (62.9 × 81.3 cm)
Jacques and Natasha Gelman Collection, Mexico

Still Life with Parrot, 1951
Oil on canvas, 10 × 11 inches (25.4 × 27.9 cm)
Harry Ransom Humanities Research Center Art Collection
University of Texas, Austin, TX (66.7)

Coconut Tears, 1951
Oil on board, 9 × 11¾ inches (22.9 × 29.8 cm)
B. Lewin Galleries, Palm Springs, CA

Coconuts, 1951
Oil on masonite, 10 × 13¾ inches (25.4 × 34.8 cm)
Collection of the Museo de Arte Moderno, Mexico City

Naturaleza Viva, 1952
Oil on canvas,
24 × 17¾ inches (61 × 45 cm)
Private Collection
Photograph courtesy of
Galeria Ramis Barquet

Still Life with Flag, 1954
Oil on masonite, 24½ × 28¾ inches (62.2 × 73 cm)
Collection of the Frida Kahlo Museum, Mexico City

Still Life with Water Melons, 1953
Oil on masonite, 15¾ × 23⅝ inches (40 × 60 cm)
Collection of the Museo de Arte Moderno, Mexico City

85

MARGINALITY AND MODERNISM

One aspect of the appeal of Kahlo to contemporary feminist cultural historians is the perceived 'marginality' of her art. The argument runs something like this. Because the centers of art history and High Art validation have been Paris and New York, and because both Kahlo's art and that of Mexico are outside this mainstream, she has a potentially important part to play in the fracturing of the predominantly Modernist account of what has been considered important in twentieth-century art. In advancing the case for her marginality, it has been usual to emphasize the folk side of Kahlo's images – to suggest that she painted using 'dialects' of naive and popular images, rather than the language of 'High Art.' Kahlo is thus pressed into a union with those Mexican and American women who, for example, have crocheted, quilted and embroidered as applied artists – women, it is argued, who have been denied access to the male-dominated world of High Art. Kahlo's art has been made to support two ends: firstly, a so-called 'radicalization' of aesthetics in order to re-order traditional art history, which is perceived as tainted with a dominant male and Eurocentric bias; and, secondly, to act as an example of a more democractic, more female, more inclusive art that embraces applied and decorative popular art. Paradoxically she is also at the same time seen to form a bridge between High Art and Applied Art.

This type of argument generally goes on to suggest that one of the most characteristic features of women's decorative arts is that it is essentially personal, private and domestic – necessarily so, it is claimed, since it has been forced into a position of isolation from public art. The analysis generally concludes with various assertions that some kind of change must inevitably take place; the marginalized and the dispossessed will cease to be private and will take their rightful place in public. Applied art, folk art, female art, will move toward center-stage. High art will be displaced or, at very least, make room for the previously lowly. In addition the past will need to be rewritten in order to take account of the hitherto unacknowledged part played by the popular arts.

What remains problematic for this cultural vanguardism, however, is the curious intractability of Kahlo's own art. While she did indeed wish her pictures to serve the revolution, it was a Communist revolution that she wanted to foster and not a radical female art and craft network. Kahlo's pictures are also *so* individual, *so* palpably egocentric, that even after making allowances for contextuality, prevailing ideology, or any of the various 'determinants' that might have circumscribed her vision, the pictures simply do not speak strongly of much other than Frida Kahlo. Her art is not easily capable of more general signification, and at best her pictures are only very crudely emblematic of other women's pain and problems. They speak most clearly about herself.

Kahlo's relationship to the European art mainstream is also far from distant, as her own links with Surrealism suggest and her own early stylistic development indicates. Her sophistication is much more evident than any genuine naivity. Kahlo was never a folk artist or a naive painter, and indeed her use of folk and popular motifs often shares with other European artists and writers of the period that faintly condescending distance that is characteristic of the conscious 'quoting' and quarrying of a distinct primitive mode.

RIGHT
Memory, 1937
Oil on metal, 15¾ × 11 inches (40 × 27.9 cm)
Private Collection

The Bus, 1929
Oil on canvas, 10¼ × 22 inches (26 × 55.9 cm)
Collection of the Dolores Olmedo Foundation, Mexico City

a dor en una salle de Detroit.

Window Display in a Detroit Street, 1931
Oil on sheet metal, 12¼ × 30 inches
(31.1 × 76.2 cm)
Mary-Anne Martin/Fine Art, New York, NY

My Dress Hangs There, 1933
Oil and collage on masonite,
18 × 19¾ inches (45.7 × 50.2 cm)
Private Collection
Photograph courtesy of Galeria Ramis Barquet

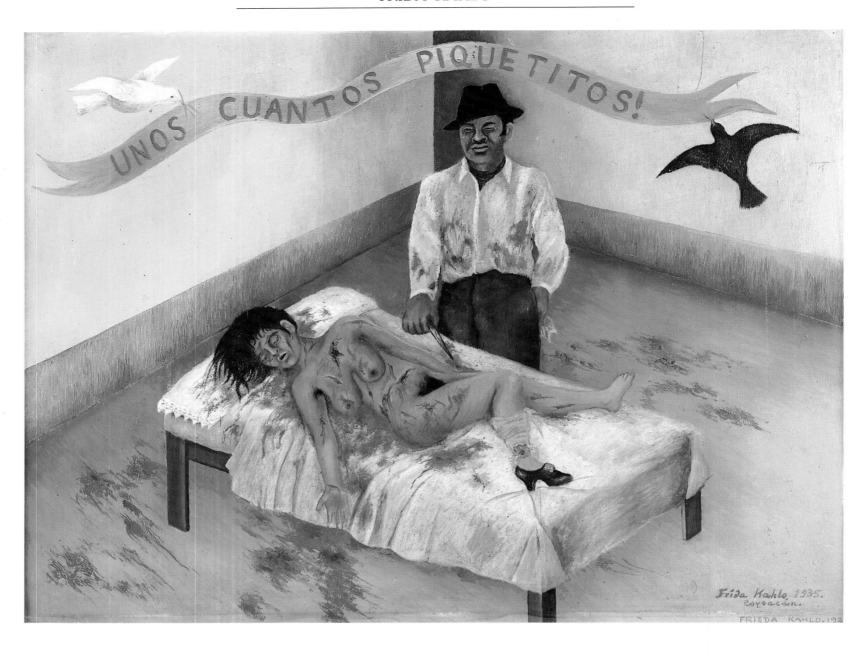

A Few Small Nips, 1935
Oil on metal, 11¾ × 15¾ inches (30 × 40 cm)
Collection of the Dolores Olmedo Foundation, Mexico City

My Nurse and I, 1937
Oil on metal, 11¾ × 13¾ inches (30.5 × 35 cm)
Collection of the Dolores Olmedo Foundation, Mexico City

What the Water Gave Me, 1938
Oil on canvas, 38 × 30 inches (96.5 × 76.2 cm)
Collection of Isidore Ducasse Fine Arts, New York, NY

The Suicide of Dorothy Hale, 1939
Oil on masonite panel with painted frame,
20 × 16 inches (50.8 × 40.6 cm)
Gift of an anonymous donor
Phoenix Art Museum, AZ (60.20)

Two Nudes in the Jungle, 1939
Oil on sheet metal, 9⅞ × 11⅞ inches (25 × 30 cm)
Mary-Anne Martin/Fine Art, New York, NY

The Dream, 1940
Oil on canvas, 29⅛ × 38¾ inches (74 × 98.4 cm)
Private Collection
Photograph courtesy of Dr Salomon Grimberg

Roots, 1943
Oil on metal, 12 × 19⅝ inches (30.5 × 49.9 cm)
Private Collection

Flower of Life, 1944
Oil on masonite, 10⅞ × 7¾ inches (27.8 × 19.7 cm)
Collection of the Dolores Olmedo Foundation, Mexico City

The Chick, 1945
Oil on masonite, 10¾ × 9 inches (27.3 × 22.8 cm)
Collection of the Dolores Olmedo Foundation, Mexico City

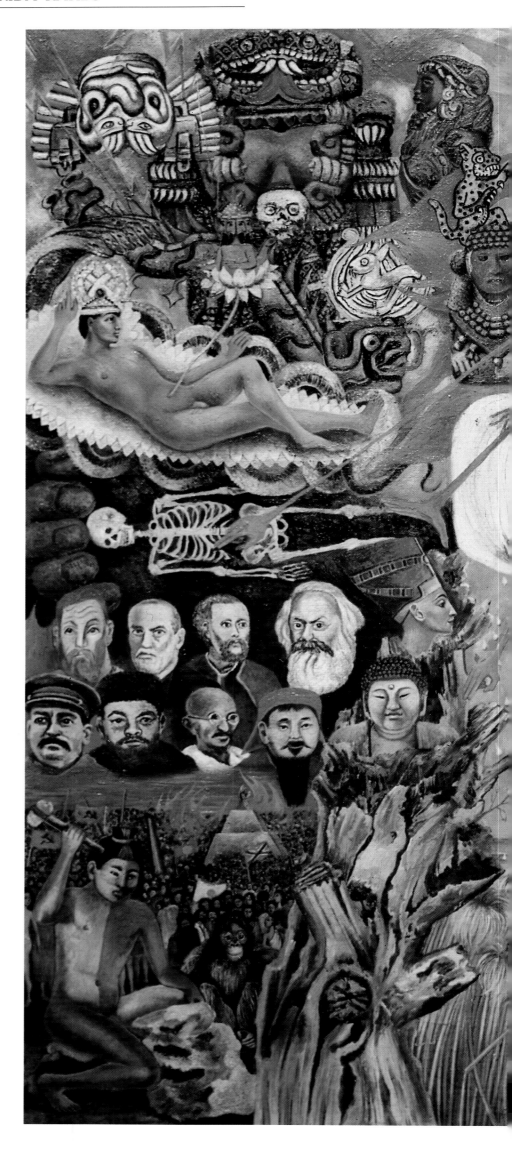

Moses, or the Seed of Creation, 1945
Oil on hardboard, 24 × 29¾ inches (61 × 75.6 cm)
Private Collection

The Little Deer, 1946
Oil on masonite, 9 × 12 inches (22.9 × 30.5 cm)
Mary-Anne Martin/Fine Art, New York, NY

The Love Embrace of the Universe, the Earth (Mexico),
Diego, Me, and Señor Xolotl, 1949
Oil on masonite, 27½ × 23⅞ inches (70 × 60.5 cm)
Jacques and Natasha Gelman Collection, Mexico

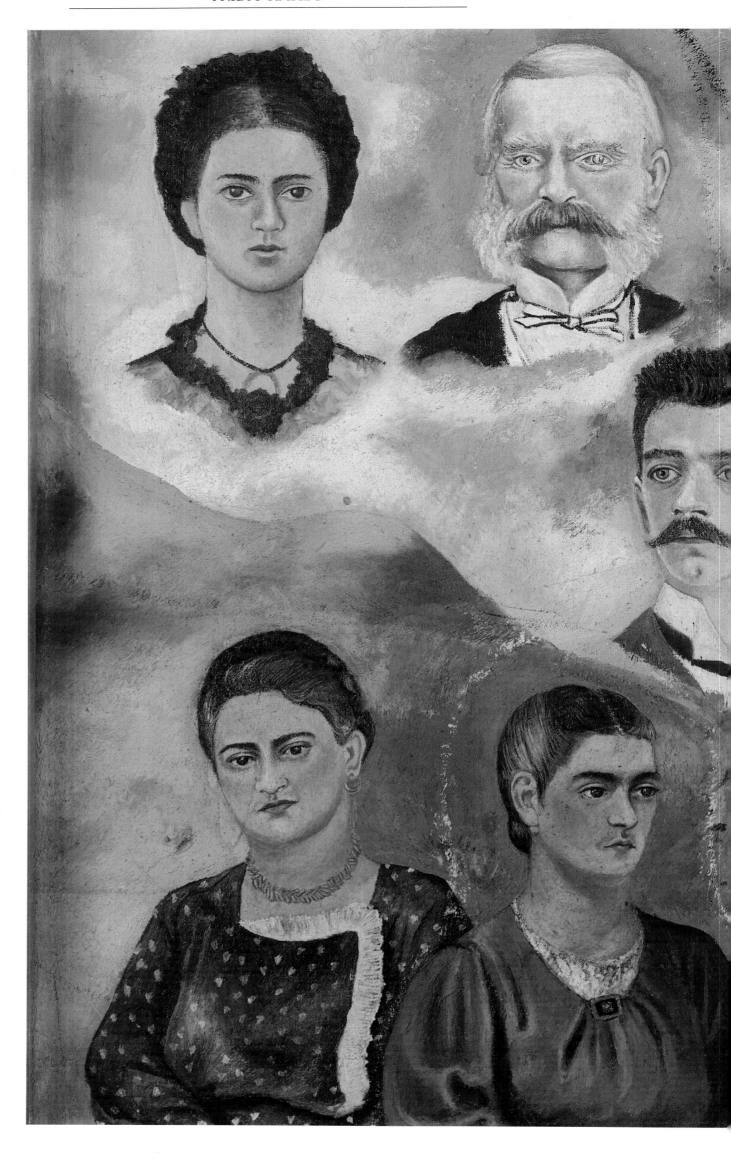

My Family, c.1949
Oil on masonite,
16 × 23¼ inches
(40.7 × 59 cm)
Collection of the
Frida Kahlo Museum,
Mexico City

ABOVE
The Circle, c.1951
Oil on sheet metal, 6 inches (15.2 cm) diameter
Collection of the Dolores Olmedo Foundation, Mexico City

RIGHT
Marxism Will Give Health to the Sick, 1954
Oil on masonite, 28¾ × 23¾ inches (73 × 60 cm)
Collection of the Frida Kahlo Museum, Mexico City

ACKNOWLEDGMENTS

The publisher would like to thank designer Martin Bristow, picture researcher Sara E. Dunphy, editor Jessica Hodge and production manager Simon Shelmerdine.

We should also like to thank the following individuals, agencies and institutions for permission to reproduce photographic material:

AKG, London: 22, 27, 62, 101, 104/105
Albright-Knox Art Gallery, Buffalo, NY: 2, 47
Berggruen Gallery, San Francisco, CA: 50
Bettmann Archive, New York, NY: 7, 17
Centre National d'Art et de Culture Georges Pompidou, Paris: 5, 45
Christie's New York, NY: 92-93
Collection of the Dolores Olmedo Foundation, Mexico City: 14 top, 26, 29, 30, 33, 34, 36, 38-39, 42, 59, 60, 61, 63, 64, 66-67, 88, 94, 95, 102, 103, 110
Collection of Idisore Ducasse Fine Arts, New York, NY: 65, 96
Collection of the Museo de Arte Moderno, Mexico City: 48-49, 81, 85
Collection of the University of California, San Francisco, School of Medicine: 35
Frida Kahlo Museum, Mexico City: 6, 9 bottom, 21, 40, 70, 84, 108, 111

Jacques and Natasha Gelman Collection, Mexico: 44, 53, 56, 57, 58, 78, 107
Harry Ransom Humanities Research Center Art Collection, University of Texas, Austin, TX: 1, 51, 79
B. Lewin Galleries, Palm Springs, CA: 80
Madison Art Center, Madison, WI: 75
Mary-Anne Martin/Fine Art, New York, NY: 31, 52, 68, 69, 76, 77, 90-91, 98-99, 106
Milner, Frank: 9 top, 10 bottom
Museum of Fine Arts, Boston, MA: 32
National Museum of the American Indian: 14 bottom
National Museum of Women in the Arts, Washington, D.C.: 43, 46
Phoenix Art Museum, AZ: 97
Private Collection (photo courtesy Dr Salomon Grimberg): 10 top, 25, 71, 74, 87, 100
Private Collection: 41, 55
Private Collection, Mexico: 82-83
San Francisco Museum of Modern Art, CA: 37
Smithsonian Institution, Washington, D.C.: 11
Sothebys, New York: 28, 73
UPI/Bettmann, New York, NY: 8 both, 12, 13, 15, 16, 18, 19, 20, 23